Yesterday Had A Man In It

Books by Leslie Adrienne Miller

Staying Up for Love
Ungodliness
Yesterday Had a Man In It

Yesterday Had A Man In It

poems by

Leslie Adrienne Miller

CARNEGIE MELLON UNIVERSITY PRESS
PITTSBURGH · 1998

Acknowledgments

Grateful acknowledgment is made to the editors of the following
publications in which these poems first appeared:

Appasionato, *Nebraska Review*
Babes in Toyland, *Prairie Schooner*
Rite of Winter, *Prairie Schooner*
Pandare, *Nimrod*
A Connect the Dots Picture, *Ploughshares*
Kebyar Trompong, *Great River Review*
Getting the Naughty Bits of *Bahasa Indonesia, Crazyhorse*
Autumnal, *Antioch Review*
Lawn Ornaments, *Crab Orchard Review*
Dark Year With Flowers, *Nebraska Review*
Valediction for an Itinerant Lover, *North Stone Review*
When Hope Goes to Hug Me, *Kalliope*
Yesterday Had a Man in It, *Crab Orchard Review*
Mermaid in the U-Bahn, *North Dakota Quarterly*
Glimpse of Germania Near Teufelsberg, *Great River Review*
Your Window on the Wannsee is Closed, *Oxford Magazine*
The Small Streets of Ubud, *International Quarterly*
Asia, *International Quarterly*
The Keening, *River Styx*
Gacela of Departed Love, *Nimrod*
Temporary Services, *Kenyon Review*
Deutcher Kaffee, *North Stone Review*
Berlin Hinterhöfe, *International Quarterly*
Die Aufklärung, *International Quarterly*

*The author wishes to thank the Goethe Institute of Chicago and
TriQuarterly for their sponsorship of a three-month fellowship at the
Literarisches Colloquium in Berlin, the Arts International Travel Grant
Program for a travel grant to Indonesia, the Minnesota State Arts Board
and the Loft McKnight Foundation for their generous support during the
completion of this book.*

The publication of this book is supported by a grant from the
Pennsylvania Council on the Arts.

PS
3563
·I4137
Y4
1998

4798-33

Contents

*The man who finds his homeland sweet is still a tender
beginner; he to whom every soil is as his native one is
already strong; but he is perfect to whom the entire world
is as a foreign land. The tender soul has fixed his love
on one spot in the world; the strong man has extended
his love to all places; the perfect man has extinguished his.*

Hugo of Saint-Victor
Didascalicon

*After all everybody, that is everybody who writes is
interested in living inside themselves. That is why
writers have to have two countries, the one where they
belong and the one in which they live really. The
second one is romantic, it is separate from themselves,
it is not real but it is really there.*

Gertrude Stein
Paris

Appasionato

Let it rest, says the cello who adores me
when the flute refuses, and I admit,

this consolation is what I sought
all along, this variation on a theme

not ardent enough. Though I shout *allegro,*
appasionato, not one of the black-gowned women

raises an eyebrow. The cello labors on
to comfort me, to say again how much he knows

I'm worth, and I turn that wealth too slowly
over to the stranger who won't dazzle my door

again. *Let it rest,* say the strings, as if
this were always the solo it's become.

I wanted the one who's lifted the silver bone
to practiced lips, blown across the right

spot, and stopped because the wind shrilling
along the sashes outside was lonelier

than any sound he could make, who lowered the flute
still warm with wrong notes, grieved that it wouldn't

thrill: breath he was ready to pour through this piece,
this place and time, air he was ready to pay

into the instrument. *Let it rest,* says the caught
breath of the man who loves what the flute refuses,

who taught the wind how to sound so wounded.

Babes in Toyland

Loring Park, Minneapolis, Minnesota

I understand why the lead singer
wears cheap yellowed lace, the A-line dress
chopped just below the hip, unhemmed,
why her hair, greeny with bleach,
glows glossy, hideous in the August twilight.
She is a studied mockery of all it has meant
to be female in the Western world,
the unreserved embrace of death itself,
agent of its own destruction, spoiled,
droll and gaudy as a plastic bead.
She can do this because she is still
baby doll pretty, petite, her bare white
legs folding like bent saplings as she spits
and fumes, mocking her own anger.
        But the drummer is another matter:
heavy, slobbering, only her feet bare
on the pedals are lovely and precise,
one ankle circled in blue tattoo,
a hardness in her calves anyone can
admire. Yet her mod print halter cuts
meaty shoulders where the orange crop
of dreadlock clashes and screeches over
rusty freckles and another pale green tattoo.

I do not understand the studied ugliness,
the small gray girls bobbing and gaping like wounded
birds in front of the stage, a grimness that is sleek
only on one or two. The rest deliberately
disheveled as rape victims, pretending the worst
has already happened to them. I know
why the beautiful, skittish ones want
to spoil their sweet mouths with ragged purple
stain, to bite their fingernails bloody
and move as though a pole were driven
clean from crown to cunt, holding them
still, screaming at the rest of us
who never suffered beauty but wanted
that cruel edge even if it was just
in part, sable drifting lashes, a round
white shoulder like a bolster a boy

could put his head on and swoon.

I'm 35 and see I have no business here,
but I can't stop wanting to be young
and I can't want enough to look as they do.
I crowd into the back where I can see
the spectacle of idiocy. Beside me a black girl,
maybe 13, lifts her baby brother up
to see the wild white kids throwing
themselves up and into the hands of strangers,
bruised, undressed as they're hauled over
the churning mass of inconsolable ennui.

I always believed dancing had something to do
with happiness, though my grandma thought
it evil, barbarous. My mother danced
anyway in the late'40s under a glittering ball,
balancing her satin wads of yellow roses
on the arms of milky boys. And I danced too
in tight jeans and halter top, summer nights
in the hometown bar, sweating, twisting,
but always smiling up at the chosen boy.
Joy was the point, we thought, or sex
eventually— you danced to prove your hips,
how you could be later, under a hand that knew
something about your body you didn't know.

But this, this agonized popping and spastic loll
of the head, ruined amethyst hair slopped
over the forehead . . . Could I have danced
like that too? Only in private, racked
on the merciless white tiles of my
bathroom, crushed and weeping when a man
I loved married elsewhere. Three days fisted
with sobs in that cold corner under the punishing
porcelain belly of the toilet, my hair
a rat of fine grief, I wanted nothing more
than to be so pitiful I'd horrify.

As they pass one girl overhead, I see
her vintage black bra under the rag of dress
plucked from some musty barrel of '40s clothes,
snap and flutter. It's a dress my mother
might have worn, a dress I too might have pulled
from a Ragstock barrel and worn in Paris
the year my lover, drunk and scrappy, threatened
to leap out a window into the Seine.

We thought we *were* happy, my mother and I,
and that's where we went wrong. These girls—
they know to wear their anger in the colors
of gems rinsed into their hair, so wrong
the topaz, jasper, ruby on strawberry blonde
minky black and ash brown. They know to tamp
the joy down so hard it has to come back
someday. Each girl knows one feature
will glow out of the cindery mess,
that the smudged yellow skin and raggy skirt
are ruin enough to suggest how well her eyes
glitter, or how her emerald streaks speak
of the dark luscious roots, exposed,
one perfect part left to adore
even though we are so near the end
that beauty is a mere scrap, a shard
of jewel which can clash and punish,
chrysolite and beryl, sardius and pearl,
gorgeous gaudiness and ornamental bathos
heaped like rotten blooms on the last vestiges
of vanity, a world of mock Ophelias,
clutching at their injured lace, desperate
and, at long last, completely safe
from the absurd and sickly sweet music
of hope.

Rite of Winter

Some evenings we scream in aerobics class—
if we feel the bass in our bones,

if the teacher goads us, if it's Friday
and January and the class is full,

suddenly, of hefty women with resolutions,
I among them, to pound away at the last

five years, the harangue of old hips.
Some of us yowl, some screech or bellow,

some even whinny— which we wouldn't do
if we thought men were looking,

but they aren't. It doesn't hurt
that there's a full moon tonight, that outside

it's 10 below, that the air is so dry
it whispers in the lungs, that it's 1994,

sex has become deadly, and the dark
cusp of the afternoon has driven us all

too far inland where we dream of the steaming
hand of a young god, joyous at hunks

of flesh so soft the hips can be cupped
like breasts. We concentrate hard

on the sure feet of the teacher, the diamond
she traces on the floor, and we count

everything: beats, calories, hours of stillness,
past lovers, those cashews on the table

where we left them. Some woman wails
You got to move, out of four speakers,

and we believe. Purple and green torsos twist
in the warped mirrors and our hundred

pairs of lungs frost the windows white.
But by the third song, we see the girl,

fresh faced as some mountain flower,
cheeks bright red with the effort

of a few steps. If she stood still
without the crutches, we'd think her lithe,

and mow her down with waves of envy,
but no, we do the laying of the eyes on her

as we, leaping and shouting, see her
come round the track on her trainer's arm,

her legs dangling like wet rags. She smiles
the whole way, knowing we're looking,

seeing us wallow down a notch. My eyes
burn a little with the possibility of tears,

or maybe just more sweat, and the roomful
of lumbering women slow, grow solemn

suddenly feeling the body go confessional.
It takes all of two stupid songs

for the girl to pass in front of us,
so we have to think about what we would do

for her, for ourselves. I think I would give
her something, wish I were generous enough

to offer my legs, but I'm not. Instead
I think I'd give her the young man

I've been watching. The winsome one who's passed
a dozen times now, circling the smiling girl

with ruined legs, circling the bunch of us
pummeling away at cloistered parts of ourselves.

The tips of her limp feet drag and catch
on the rubber track. Our heels come down

harder. The boy with the fair face
I was willing to give up must have caught

the drift of my thought, of our many desires
rising in the steam of sweat and self-flagellation,

for he was the loveliest of the evening's
runners, the one whose face really made us shout

in the first place, whose glossy chest exploded
with doubling and tripling in the mirrors.

Now, he is gone, and the girl who made us suddenly
think of sacrifice falls back hard

into her wheelchair near the glut machines.
As we come to the last hamstring stretch, we hope,

we pray, we won't have to see her now
in the locker room, naked, crushed, and thin

beyond belief, evidence of just how much
punishment the rest of us so richly deserve.

Pandare

His heart must have been bad for years, maybe even before
he came to me, a gift from my then lover
who saw how I bent down for wild cats in the street
and spoke to their silence the way and words
the lover himself had wanted to hear.
Thirty dollars bought him life as a fixed Tom,
and me an animal who would last through two more,
almost three, men. He helped me find the chosen ones:
when they wouldn't do, he hid, when they would
he roamed the edges of the bed, my stranger,
my conscience, the collective temper of my sex
wandering outside the body as it falls under
the pleasure of love. And I loved the ones
who loved the cat, the knowledge in the way
their hands moved over him moved over me.
Ten years before the muscle around his heart,
swollen, knocked against his ribs, crushed
the blood in its moving, and left one leg cold.
The last, the chosen lover, not loved enough,
rocked him between us in the space where there was nothing
but the small jazz of animal breathing.
He taught the cat to take treats out of his ears,
his navel, from the small rise of his Adam's apple,
even at the end, from between his teeth,
the little block of dried liver,
that even dying, the cat desired.
Now he is ashes, shards of bone and tooth
we would like to divide between us and carry
for different reasons into the days ahead.
The last time we tried to touch each other
we knew he wouldn't last, we feigned sleep
to watch him pull himself out of the bends
in our elbows, out of shadow that shared
his color, out of the space we made,
and steal across the room in all the manner of hunt
he knew, silver head lifted to catch the scent,
the cooling pile of trousers and shirt tossed
across a chair back. When he found the part
he wanted, sweet with sweat, he took it in his mouth,
tugging till it all fell in a murmur of embrace.

16

A seam in his teeth, a piece under each paw,
a trill of luxury in his throat, he began
the ritual of kneading and pulling,
the pink knot of his genitals exposed, leaking
its scant milk, giving himself, even dying,
giving himself to the rich abandon of another.

A Connect the Dots Picture

Zanesville, Ohio

The pine tree at the corner of the lot
where my childhood home, a ranch house,
sits like a snapped sugar wafer on a slope.
Tents in Upton's field collapsed and pushed
aside for a game of kickball or just tumbling.
The oldest Upton girl whom I adore,
nearer adulthood than I, her head in a sky
I cannot but wish to see. *Follow me,*
she says, *I will show you something really neat.*
And I go up the stone path and stairs
among the lolling day lilies and ivy
behind the marvelous girl to a place
nested in trees where a garden hose
uncoils in her hand. *There,* she says,
holding the metal rimmed end to my face.
I must be nine, possibly ten. I love Christy.
She taught me to make ice cream in a bucket.
She combed my hair as if I were a doll.
She took my hand and led me away from the gang
of boys in the field where I tried so hard
to be good and strong. *There,* she says tenderly,
look in there, and I cast my whole being
into her command. Some wonder is about
to happen in the dark hole of the hose.
Sputter of laughter, and more laughter,
and I realize I cannot see her, or anything.
There has been a blast of air, water. I think
I am crying and hope not. In this world
tears have never been good. Once, when Casey cried,
his sister forbad me to tell anyone, ever,
and she smacked him till he stopped.
But now my face is wet, my hair, my loose
summer shirt which I like more than all the others
in my drawer because it has two girls on it,
hand in hand, and they wear shirts exactly
like this one. No, I am not sobbing. Good.
But I am cold, and my eyes sting.
I try to look where Christy was and may
still be when the smarting stops. She is trying
to teach me something adult. Complicated.
How it feels to be stung by the force

of your own desire turned back on you,
and the possible responses: regret or fury.
One day I will understand that one is antidote
to the other. Years later in the darkening room
of a country not my own, real history heaped
in the corners, I stand next to a man
who has just begun to be weary of my hopefulness,
unwavering desire that simply asks for it.
His is a small travesty, a forgotten promise
that left me waiting all of an afternoon.
Smell of wet stones, gnats hovering
around the spigot dribble. My shirt has not
been ruined, Christy clucks, unnerved at this kid
who stands in mute trust, dripping, comic,
obscenely forlorn. This was not the point.
She meant to send me screaming like any child,
home— but home, if ever I had one
is on another continent, inching away.
The man draws back from the insipid scene,
unpleasant female disappointment gathering
in his room, ruining the evening, filling his shoes,
making the air too close. The offending garden hose
settles far under the ivy, and it is intolerable
that I should keep standing here expectantly,
taking it, asking for more, still too much
in love. It was that, then, that Christy wanted
to wash from my face. In the long minute
of my blindness, the summer afternoon went
cruelly on in my ear. A horsefly. The dog
somewhere itching itself. Smack
of the rubber ball against a boy's toe
down in the field. Small shush of ivy
where the hose falls. Drips on the stone.
It's only water, dummy, she says, disgusted.
I look straight into her eyes and she sees
she hasn't gotten rid of it, that appalling
ardor. Too much of something sticky, serious,
and she hates me for it.

Kebyar Trompong

Ubud, Bali

The kebyar dancer touches each nippled gong,
a whole row of brass breasts singing

under his wand, his eyes shifting coyly
this way, then that. A girl joins him,

shuffling sideways in the tube of her gold
sarong. Frangipani blossoms moor

in her inky hank of hair and tatter
with her moving. The two dancers wriggle

together and down to the floor, hips
almost, almost fused, then no, not quite:

he's defined a space, she pushes through its pink
degrees. He and she entwine the humid curves

of possible contact and teeter apart,
leaving the force of desire in the air

above the floor, at the edge of the slope
smothered in morning glories: *Many white people,*

says the guide, *have slipped off
this edge, plunged straight down*

not knowing what the vines hide—
thickets of green tangle and bite

under which there may be gods, screaming
women, teeth of the wood, slim fast snakes

and the spider waiting her turn
in among the golden scales, tendrils,

plumes. *Tomorrow we will offer a pig,
a goat, a dog and a hen,* he says hopefully.

*And when we have cockfighting, I come
for you.*

Household Shrines

. . . although specific types of shrines are required in every compound, it is often not clear— even to the Balinese who set offerings there every day— exactly to whom and for what purpose the shrine has been erected.

Bali: Sekala & Niskala

She wants to do the magic on me, and I
allow her to try. Though emptiness like mine
is vast as the gape of sky above the Sayan gorge,
and my flesh has shrunk to a web, my hair,
damp and blonde to limp strings, she wants
to touch the bone of my nose, to soften the blades
of my turning in the sheets leaden with dew.
I cannot make my love over to her, which is all
the reason she gives hers like the offerings each day,
to me, small baskets sewn in the night and given,
given again, trampled in the morning, hibiscus
petals crushed and strewn, incense reduced to cool
dust. She never finds the gift, the charmed
confluence of some new word, flower, color or curl
of landscape I crave. The mountains have worn
a sash of mist ever since we came, and held apart
the views she promised. *Today*, she says,
today, you can take the picture. I give nothing
back but clear large eyes, blue of the shallows
which swallows all kindness. At home, men call this
melancholy, but we're not men, and I'm not home.
Whoever will please me pleases stone, residence
of the gods, perhaps, but who knows if they
are home today. Whoever tries to tend me tends
only dissolution. When it rains I'm sullen as ash.
When it's dark I'm sullen as water. When
she gives me red wine in the jungle evening,
I laugh a little and leave her. She wants
my heart, and I hand it over gladly because
it wants shaping, and I'm tired of trying to do it.
I sleep away from her, away from the window,
propped open for me on a view of the gorge.
In half dark and cock crowing I forsake her
every day, creep downstairs to remake her

and a world about which I know nothing.
She wanted to go back for my umbrella left
in the sill of the toilet near the palace
from which Sukarno watched Balinese women
bathing nude and picked the ones he wanted to bed.
She knew I didn't like to get wet. Rain and moss
eat the soft stone walls and shrines in mere months.
I am that gray place where her offerings rot,
even though one jeweled eye is open over the basket
of rice and flowers. The boys start sweeping
at first light, the coconut-spine brooms hissing
across packed mud, collecting all the downed, browned
blossoms, pollen, sticks and dead bees,
the bodies of small red spiders that bite hard,
residue of all the lamps I wanted lit last night,
their wicks now curled and shed like insect wings.
With the dawn, I can't see that the lamps are still
burning, still sipping their thin, yellow oil,
but I smell them: low black smoking
over the empty bottles of French wine
she brought here just for me.

Getting the Naughty Bits of Bahasa Indonesia

Jakarta

Saras is the one who finally agrees to give me
the word they say old ladies spit when caught
by surprise, then deny having spoken, having
ever even known. It's *vulgar* she says passing me
the cocktail napkin, folded twice, the ugly word
pinched, and shoved under the table like a bribe.
Umi and Isma titter and twist their hair,
wondering just what this *boule* girl wants
with the nasty word. *Burung*, warns Sita, is nicer,
acceptable among women, but the other
we never say. I'm the guest tonight, who must,
in proper Javanese fashion, be indulged
no matter how tactless my request. The word
they take so long to give up looks innocent enough,
resting in print like the member it names
until roused by the tongue, the throat, air
forced out of the body in an effort at speech.
From its glottal launch through the open
vowel of *bother* and *hot*, the hum at the center
and long loll of its second moaning vowel,
it tangles our tongues, though no one has dared
actually speak it. Any old lady will say it
if you scare her suddenly, they all agree— as if
she's jolted awake at the thought of the thing.
Sweet Jesus, my grandmother murmured
when I burst at her with headlong girlish vim—
Burung means *bird*, says Saras, and I imagine
a flock of ruddy penises standing up,
taking wing at the narrow sky. The five women
nod conspiratorially: *If you have to say
something* . . . but they wonder what I plan
to do with these words the few days I have left
in this country. Will I be asking to see any *burungs*?
Saras wonders, eyebrows raised, chewing the pen
from whence this other, the unseemly, word came.
Add an "r" and it's a harmless English word,
though my question's a travesty from which these women
will take the wrong impression: she's curiously crude,
this American girl who wants such a word, who refolds it
carefully like a love note, a naughty bit she'll
take with their names, the scales of their laughter,

home, where it will lie in a drawer with photos
of this table, fruit markets, rice terraces, mossy
statues of their gods, and someday when her mind
is all broken toys and dust, she'll find it,
like the children she's never had leaping from a closet
to frighten her, and she'll spill it without thinking,
this word she's never said aloud before, this forbidden
tidbit that will mean nothing in the middle of America,
nothing, this crass little beast of a word
that now, she can never unknow.

At the Bandung Emergency Room
Bandung, Central Java, Indonesia

After I refused the doctors in Hong Kong
and Jakarta, after fever knocked on all the doors
in my blood for fourteen days and nights,
I agreed. A., furious with worry
as my head lolled and bobbed beside her
in the back seat of her Peugeot, took
my hot skull into her lap, raked her brown
fingers in my blonde hanks of damp hair—
You're afraid of our doctors, maybe,
not a question but an answer.
I search my scorched circuitry for the why—
because whatever pokes now through the drawers
of my blood must be safer than what waits
in the waiting room, gluey strings of bacteria
on the chairs, the air a kaleidoscope of germs
my sterile western veins have never touched.
I'm not sick enough for a doctor, I say,
believing that if my body heals itself,
I'll be one of you. What I have came with me
from Hong Kong, before I knew my need
could colonize, came with the bowl
of hot noodles and squid I took that first
night in Asia, gift of the woman who slid
her hand across her own hot breath
and set the bowl before me, steaming—
here, her hands said, here is the heat
you came for, here is the way to live
in the storm of possible contagions;
take my small killable germs and let them
ingratiate you to whoever you meet
elsewhere in back streets, villages;
here is a mask of distress by which
they will know and love you.

And I accepted the soup, the squid gummy
and good going down, and I held on to its heat
all the way to Bandung where the rain
talks all afternoon and mold crawls
up the walls, dark wherever one touches,
fills the chinks knocked in tiles around

the sink, where yet another chicken soup
arrives with the man who will fix the toilet,
yellow rags of skin bobbing in the broth
and stippled with pocks where the feathers
were yanked. All of Asia has tried to mend me,
but I can't eat. I sleep fantastically
in the fever's busy in and out, hiss
of bare feet in the night, A. watchful,
and the long monotone prayers from the mosque
burning in among words I speak in my sleep.
A., I tell you now I thought I held my fever
to me like a flower from a possible lover,
a way to etch the strange country more deeply,
to char a path of knowing into the grooves
of my weak memory. I come from a country
of drinkable water and curable mysteries.
But here, affliction is the easiest way
around difference. Because I am permanently
pale, your blonde doll, your beleaguered
traveler, because there is no way for me
to turn my hot gaze on your world
without changing it, I must give up
my fever, and you your ministry; we must
leave it here in the Bandung *Rumah Sakit*,
house of sickness, where even the light
is green and weary, and the nurse's
much-washed dress is a map on which
all the webs of the day's emergencies
finally connect.

Autumnal

Isle of Happy Days, Mikana, Wisconsin

Autumn, so you stand in a blood bath of leaves and light,
    summer cut to pieces and floating its tossed scarves
    on the burnished water and away from the spit of land
    where you stand, unsmiling, confused. I'm a woman
    gone mean in the season's turn.

The switch you snap from among the bent grass
    is ruby red and limber as a long-legged girl,
    the switch that I catch as you flick at a stone
    and think of my bare knee. I dig the stick
    from your grip and swat your woolly curls,
    brighten at the good suck-whap when it lifts
    the shirt from your back, bites your open neck.

It feels too good hitting you out here,
    where anyone could see but no one does. Another two
    in Ivy League sweatshirts step out of the woods, say "Hi,"
    and stumble away when they see. The end
    of the land is ours, we say with the stare that sends
    them off.

I hurt you and hurt you because the stick is red
    and made for this. You snap a new one and sit in a ball
    wanting to look small, pitiable, a way to fight fighting
    back. But I am crazy dancing now, one foot up the hill
    one foot down, going for the cheek you've turned. I get
    your ear's soft rim red.

Autumn, and Saturday, so there's all the time in the day,
    and nothing we want with words. Nothing the punch
    of light can't say, cool air slapping welts in the lake
    until we tire and carry our marks back to the quaint
    room, the lodge restored to turn of the century luxury,
    a bed we rent at a price that could buy our own.

We lie in the afternoon after, the red
    sticks captured each from the other and tossed to the lake.
    I want you to want me but not too much, so we enter
    the dining room and find our place before the last edible
    flowers flung over the meat's dark hip, and no one
    thinks twice about the welt on my neck, or yours.

The owner's girl who knows what she is
    in a tight tee, carries her nipples like pistols
    before the rest of her blonde walking into the dining
                                   room's
    clutter of middle-aged couples in madras and seersucker.
    She leads a pack of yellow-haired girls in low riding
    jeans. They've been sleeping out on the island
    where their bras hung like bandages among the trees.

You register her presence, squirm against your
    tennis shorts, and see again the white, sweet leavings
    in the trees, the teen magazines, glossy and gaudy
    as the turned leaves above, squashed chip bags,
    and everywhere the musty smell of freshly ovulating girl,
    girl you shouldn't want, but do, and why I had to
    hurt you out there on the furthest point of land,
    why I had to drive you down, hands before your face,
    whimpering and regrettably aroused, to the water's
    very edge.

Picture Hat

Jeff Koons Exhibition Opening
Walker Art Center, Minneapolis

Just before sunset, I drive the high deck
of freeway and praise my good luck at catching
the gold spikes over the skyline, gilt running
down the river that cuts the cities' circle
like a wide diagonal no, and when I come down
at Lyndale, smoke gauzes the ramp, snakes
around downtown and tightens like a bracelet.
Light that a moment ago was gold, now dries
pale and brittle as straw, and I smell it,
a big fire, close. Something old and old
is burning down. I fight the primal pull
to follow the smoke, which I see now boiling
from Uptown, a dirty white trumpet of ash,
and though I see no flame, the city
is suddenly hot. Sirens die in the distance,
and I hear a whole block of warehouses
roaring down in my childhood town, see
the fathers wide-eyed, as ancient interiors
eat themselves alive. "Arson," someone
whispers later at the opening where we've all
come to view the explosions of Ilona's white
backside and gawk at the gaudy bears and bunnies
stiffened in silver and cased by a crowd
dressed to kill. Arson, or not, my friend
and I in our black art opening dresses
and picture hats, our sparkling reticules
and molded hair, should have gone to the fire
itself. We should have gone to hear
the orange tongues singing the end
of the sweatshop where forty Asian women
worked dull scissors in burning hands.
Instead, we posed with our Perrier
on the marble stairs, by the dried roses
and arched windows of the Marcel Arms,
preened and smooched at the dry air,
and went on laughing to the show of art,
pushed our black hips in among the others,

reached for the soft bellies of stuffed
mushrooms, skewered fruit and the inky
bubbles of berry garnish that stained
our fingertips and teeth. "Fire"
and "Streets Closed" say the Xeroxed signs
the guards tape over glass way out
of the galleries, so we take our hatted
heads to the upper terrace where the smoke
hangs low under a spit of rain in the dark.
Somewhere in the galleries, the artist strolls
in a white tux, his wife beside him,
the Italian porn queen herself, beaded
and radiant to her gold stilettos.
Lightning silvers the west, and the Basilica
whitens on the other side of the sculpture garden,
its façade as gaudy and intricate as Ilona's
creamy calves in white fishnet, her white hair
wreathed in flowers and spilled from her ceramic head.
They hold their baby toward the painted cherubs
giggling down on so much white flesh,
and the fire eats the humid air, moans,
and a fine sweat crawls over the peachy lips
of a man in a blonde wig bending over a silver
blow-up rabbit. Something old and old
is burning down. A suited man tells a woman
with blazing hair that he hasn't done openings
since he met his current wife. Now he's looking
for a new model, staring into the clean long
faces of Hoovers in lighted glass cases.
I peer out from under the black brim
of my grandmother's hat at the artist's prim
penis, blown up and grainy, the size
of a man's shoe. It lies there politely,
not quite unfurled, but large as the head
of the man who once owned it. I adjust
my black hat and think of the other hats
I might have worn, the few dozen best
saved from grandmother's house, a red
winged velvet, the black lacquered plate
with veil and plumes, all what never

saw the likes of this, a generation come
to sacrifice a heaven of white flesh and gilded
porcelain, where it's no good to be good,
and not good enough to be bad, so we
wander coolly through hell's burning closet
of black dresses, red lips and deadly
disaffection, refuge, however small,
from the blinding kitsch of sweetness
and light.

Lawn Ornaments

Zanesville, Ohio

The first time I stood in the charged air
of female rage, I didn't know that night
would always have something to do with it,
that if anyone ever kissed you so your blood
lurched into your throat and your new body
leaked and burned, and then tried to pretend
it never happened, you'd have to get them
back. That's what must have happened to Alice
and why she needed seven girls
in someone's father's finned Buick
careening through the spring night
like the gray weight of a mother possum,
babies packed away in her pockets.

At first we meant only to filch a few
pink flamingos and dump them in his yard.
Whatever the boy had done, we didn't need
to know. We let her anger lead us, choose one
of our names each time we'd circled
the block enough to be sure the take
was right: terribly grinning elves,
a whole family of tactless yellow ducks,
plastic pinwheels that would snap
and hiss with a little wind.
We couldn't tell from the street
how heavy they were, how many girls
it would take to carry the hunched
and crude creature that turned out
to be a plaster lamb. And we didn't
anticipate the pill bugs, the wet worms
that clung to its underside, dropped
through the gaps in our blouses
as we ran screeching to the car. Alice
drove, welcomed us each back into the musty
interior of the Buick now filling with
drying dirt, grass clippings and edges
of molded plastic sharp as her own
laughter at the boy's dark house,
a street where no lawn ornament
ever winked an exaggerated eye.

It isn't over yet, our imperviousness
to adult pain, but we can taste the fakeness
of it like the smell of wet plastic
in the car, chewed baby toys, dolls left out
overnight so their skin fades and stinks.
Alice's rage has filled our laps,
our ears, and we are laughing back, someone
has even peed her pants a little because
the curved neck of a pink flamingo has snapped
in the wind of our flight. She dangles
the wet bulb over the seat like a puppet,
the head of the boy we're helping Alice kill.

We're crammed so tight among the mushrooms,
leprechauns and giant spiky flowers
underfoot, we crush and crack the ducks,
fling out cartoon daisies, dump the swollen
ladybug with stupid surprised eyes.
We tangle the flamingos by their awful
hooked necks and pour all the dented
characters of our childhood stories
into the yard of the boy we can't
really hurt.

When you're a girl, rage and shame
have the same sinister, too-bright smile,
and that perfectly shaved blue hill
is the body of all the men who will
make you feel it. You'll have to run
across that moonless expanse in secret,
armed with laughter, and girls who'll help you
make that yard crazy with cuteness,
girls who'll fill the smashed grin
of the garden dwarf with someone's tube
of Poppy Pink and jam him upside down
in a bed of plastic roses.

Dark Year With Flowers

Baltimore, Maryland

In that year it seemed we were only alive
at night, the yellow boat lights girlish
and woozy with the harbor's billow and slosh.
You worked at the water's edge all evening,
black trousers, black vest, a white towel over
your forearm to wrap the sweating bottles
of wine poured for patrons, while I, up the hill,
scribbled in a small lagoon of lamplight.
At three, a trickle of brightness spilled
in with you from the hall, and I'd rise
to your bumble in the kitchen fishing
soggy wads of dollar bills from your pockets
to the table. If there were sprays of flowers
in the stalls that year, we couldn't
afford them, but we found their likeness
in fabrics from the mill where ends
were a buck a yard. Together we carried
away bolts of printed chrysanthemums, iris,
tea roses, and clothed the tall windows,
the tub, the soiled couch, the splintered table
saved from the alley. Now, I could buy
my own real flowers, as could you,
but you won't arrive again in the wee hours,
drunk and maudlin, some of the bills
lost from your pockets, a vague smell
of blood and dust in your hair, and no idea
what trouble you'd met beyond your own self-loathing.
And I can no longer elude my instinct
for self-preservation, rise on my elbow
and love again the beery shadow in the doorway,
shirtsleeves still rolled and glowing
in that little rift of light we couldn't
swathe with long panels of nodding mums.
I can no longer reach for the cold stem
of the Stolychnya bottle you've pulled
from the freezer and offered me
like an impulsive gift of live blooms.

Past Perfect

Shrink, shrank, shrunk, have, had, and will have
shrunk, we sang out somewhere in adolescence,

liking the sheer poetry of correctness,
of *helping verbs*— before *shrink* became noun,

before *mental illness,* before anyone I knew
needed *help,* and *shrink* meant simply

nouveau riche, twenty years before
I understood that to understand the self,

to question the done deal of the past
was to need every tense I had ever learned,

and then some, before I entered the clean
private room with afternoon sunlight gouging out

a special seat for me, a box of Kleenex
offering itself on the small table between

me and the woman I paid to go figure
my days. *Shrink, shrank, shrunk,* I sang

coming or going, pleased that at last
I understood what they did, which wasn't

so much: *to dwindle,* yes, *to draw together*
or contract from the heat, moisture or cold

of one's own acts. She lead me only to the best
vantage points, white cliffs really, from which

I could contemplate safely the vast green
ravine of childhood, the powerful mother

riding through my particular forest, bow
and arrows ready, the father standing outside

one of the nicer huts, trimming his mustache
in the basin's dark mirror. There I am too,

lying in ambush for my mother, proud
of the trap I've laid for her, the pit trap

she taught me to make in the earthy heart
and which she invariably evades. You see,

I was often distracted by young boys slipping
through the forest on their strong toes,

naked to the waist, chests oiled with sweat.
I should have been one of them and blamed

my mother . . . but my story is so very old,
the same story many of us tell and which

my shrink already knows. We find more
wood to feed the great fire in her clean

little room, the brocade sofa where I sit,
picked clean at the edge by many manic

fingers. I pride myself on never having reached
for the temptation of Kleenex between us.

My mother taught me to keep my tears to myself.
My father whispered, *Go ahead, weep.*

The world grew up while I wasn't looking,
my forest suddenly insane with new houses,

still smelling of fresh plaster, plush carpets,
and filling with shrinks for every ill, there,

the shrink for anger, for the child, for marriage,
for death, for birth, for the sting of love,

for sex or no sex, the shrink of excessive yearning,
the shrink of envy and agony, shrink of simple pain.

Even the boys I'd chased with lust in the old
forest, grew up, became shrinks themselves,

and married: *to draw back, to recoil,*
and so I did, but never admitted anything

of the sort to Her, my stony priestess
perched on her overstuffed chair, so intent

on my answers, dark pupils unreadable.
Laugh, damn it, laugh, I said in code,

I have done, had done and will have done.
Isn't it funny, funny, how much it hurts?

She didn't even blink, the cruel bitch.
I have been in love with one of you,

I said to her with my eyes. *Guess it, come on,*
guess it, and I'll trust you forever. Of course,

she never guessed, and I left that city suddenly,
came north where shrinks, I thought, were scarce,

land like my green old one, flat and full
of earnestness, self-reliance blooming

like wild roses on every face. I draw
the cape of memory back around my shoulders,

spend whole afternoons alone, conjuring
those boys on ponies, those savage days.

The only boon at last was to lie down
in a field of snow with a shrink who was once

one of those boys. *Why didn't you carry me*
away long ago? I ask his hips with mine.

Why didn't we hide in the trees and fight
those who came to build there? Sleek boy

that you were, were we not better ill?
Sunlight pours over the middle of my life

this morning. The untouched box of white tissue
ignites, and the woman with blank eyes nods,

Yes, yes, time is up, and I rise awkward
as the teen I have been for the last hour,

and will be a few hours more, opening
momentarily in the dark pit trap of my own

making, mothered and fathered with my lover
before he was a lover, before grammar, before

the simple past turned back on itself
and conspired against its own perfection.

Whale Watching

Baja, Mexico

Here the ragged desert climbs into the sea,
rough elbows and knees of buttes jutting up
from both coast and ocean floor, a gray thread
of road bent above the line of surf. Shall we say
that we saw them, the whales, whole and beautiful
in all their tons of flesh? Or will we tell
the truth: there was only one whale, and though
we know it was large as a house, we saw no more
than the gray ridge of its back floating up,
a little spout of water, and then only roiling
ocean again. It might be better to tell
of the pair of dolphins circling the elusive
ballena, how impossibly perfect their timing
as they arced, circled and defined the giant arena
of spectacle. I'm plotting this story with a woman
so like myself I've stopped thinking for two.
A man we both almost, but not quite loved,
led us to know each other and is now gone
under both our lives— or rather, he's a story
we share and embellish, emblem of our matched
pasts, even without him, too much alike. Now
we've both escaped from new beaus for a week,
Baja in the off season. Wind has overturned
umbrellas and ruffled the manes of horses,
shaggy, fat and bored on the beach.
The light, bright and sharp, catches
our twinned blonde heads. We climb
to the upper deck of the pitching boat
bulbous with orange life jackets, cameras
ready, scan the empty sea for a glimpse,
already sure of how it will appear, an oily fin,
a rolling eye, but the wind's the only marvel
out here, sweeping miles into the sky's vast maw,
so we fall to fathoming the shapes of lives
we've left at home, far inland and north
where winter this year, is more brutal
than usual, the men we've left behind,
too new yet to mythologize. I give her what
there is, the story of mine, rigid, beautiful,
spare and kind to a fault, and she gives me

the story of hers, impulsive, wounded
and frank about what he wants, what he
cannot give. We'd like to take these men,
awash in the perfect circle of our fictions,
and make them into one magnificent creature
both careful and careless, reticent
and candid, paragon of patience and ruin
of impatience, but however long we look
we see only the small part of them visible
above water. We don't even know what gifts
to bring them, our princes of possibility—
Cuban cigars, Prozac, Guatemalan chocolate,
or mescal with a worm? We keep turning
to the story we do know, the man who brought us
together, and is now another woman's elusive
subject, though for us he's gone and nothing,
but complete enough to imagine wholly, our creation,
our story, our great gray monster of the deep.

Valediction for an Itinerant Lover

Cantabit vacuus coram latrone viator.
Travel light and you can sing in the robber's face.
                                    Juvenal

When you get to Rio, I'll be relieved,
free of all this prickly suspicion

you're not rapt enough about my knees,
my range of hills so sparsely populated

the dogs have gone wild again. Nice
scenery, perhaps, but no one has died

on these beaches for centuries,
and the last time I threw myself

from a cliff, the sea returned me
as casually as a silk scarf. But your

boat happened just outside the harbor,
and we know you were looking for kisses.

Whatever you are, the wind hasn't
yet told us, but we've seen your shadow

unraveling the world's watery edge,
like the day the moon went before

the sun, and there were moments
of darkness we couldn't use.

So it happened the first time you came.
When you took the view and pronounced

it lovely, we thought so too, primeval
continent that we are— lakes

you've never entered, blue as eggs
of birds you've never heard,

deep as the paths we've made through
the hushes and sighs, green

as any fancy. Go on to some tropical
place if you must. We'll be here

when you return, but know what your
wending undoes. We'll be deeper

in our old nests, heavy as brook stones.
We'll have made our crude snares

and hidden our prettiest babies.
We don't trust ourselves completely,

and though we hope to sleep the whole way,
we'll probably end up singing.

When Hope Goes to Hug Me

Lunged into her, my long arms stiff
from lack of this, I'm surprised how brittle,
how far gone I am. When did it end,
the ease of reaching, the circle
we mother to bring a body in? She
is distant as a film I watch,
figures from another country, fluid
in the mind, formal in the flesh. They
and she are on the other side of a glass,
a lens, a strip of tiny images, but the arm
comes in, hard and real so it frightens
all the birds in the cages of my bones.
She is pregnant, and I've been wanting
to touch the hard jar of belly,
thinking of how it would roll
under my palm, but now that she's here
clapping the old boat of me into her,
I remember the way the seed must
have found its wet mark, and the man
who launched it without full agreement.
Like me, perhaps he was shocked
by the breadth of her hug, the smell
of damp life in her hair, her toes,
all of her a place to swim, to drink,
to wash the winter's dead skin off.
She floats like her child on hope
but he's busy drawing lines
she cannot cross, lines like mine
that fall from the places on our bodies
where they're etched by days and years,
thin necklaces of flesh that we pull
from our throats and cast down to keep
the young out, to keep them from
pushing their tumescent limbs too
close. The seeds she stole from
that dry tangle of leaf and branch
were meant to die, to lie in the flake
and dust of wintry air— as my own skin,
chalky from forced air heat and dazzle
of sunlight on snow, no longer knows

how to let her near. I cook her dinner
and keep a distance, the child more
plausible in my head than in her belly.
When she leaves me I haven't touched
it as I meant to, fully, holding the whole
bulb of it in my palm. I want to, but when
her hug comes forward, her fecund breath
lifts my papery hair, my ribs rattle,
my knees lock, and I see the way I'll sleep
tonight, tomorrow and the next, the dull
book of my thighs clapped shut, my bones
folded over my heart, my womb a wrap
I've had to cast out and around me
to stay warm.

Yesterday Had A Man In It

Linum, Germany

How many times might it happen
in one woman's life that a man,
a surprisingly bright and nice-looking man,
gives her the gift of a day in the country—
preferably a foreign country— and shows her
something— an animal, a church, a cave,
something about which he has a story?
Often there are remarkable flowers involved,
rain keeps to itself, and many more
colors of green are discovered
than anyone believed there could be.
Three times? Five times? Ten?
Perhaps there was even a lake, a small
boat they could rent, a fisherman
whose line they caught by accident
and angered. Complicitous giggling, oars
dipped among the closing nubs of lilies.
Of course, it could as easily have been
a raw landscape, a yellow mountain
of rocks flat and clinking like plates,
an icy lake that reflected someone's recent
past, though it's not yet time to speak
of that. Rather, they examine
tracks and leavings the man can match
to a marvelous creature, another story.
But surely it was an apple orchard, autumn,
where there were bees he wanted to explain,
seven kinds of apples, sliced, browning,
sticky, and he said they might lie down
under a tree, speak to the sky.
This happened to someone at least once,
a luckier woman many times— or unlucky
if you believe this is a kind of hope
that rarely finds its mark. Empty
fairgrounds, abandoned airstrips, a field
bruised with some remarkable event,
the usual parks. One luminous glance
and the hope returns like a trained bird,
the light diffused around its homing,
the air around the kiss she gets

brief and sweet and almost real,
so later she can sleep in the thought
of it— yes, that bud may open tomorrow—
though tonight she'll wake confused
by the momentary odor of otherness,
her own hair buried in the pillow.

Mermaid in the U-Bahn Station

We have not seen her in two days,
the pale Aryan with luscious bare breasts
who swung her tail of sparkling scales
over a rock in every station in Berlin.
How they thought she'd sell cigarettes
with her unearthly gift of chest
I do not know, but I yearned myself
toward those two milky knobs,
their painted rusty nipples,
couldn't take my eyes away when the train
rolled over my view of her and tore
the veil of my reverie. "There are,
you've noticed, two versions of her,"
my woman friend remarks, and I realize
we've both been drinking deeply at the image.
Protective, indignant, we want to stand
between her and the sticky pleasure
of every man waiting for a train
and feasting on her creamy reflection.
But I never saw a man openly take
his pleasure from her as we did,
coveting and wishing to cover her at once.
How many times now have I gone over her
in my mind, the impossible heft and curve
of those breasts like balloons of water
thrown and shaped momentarily by the force
of air, caught in that brief moment before
they fall and spray. How long before
I noticed the woman herself at all,
her delicate collar bone, her polished
shoulders, impassive pale face
and handfuls of moon-colored hair?
She stared upward at every *Bahnhof* ceiling
away from the swarthy boy smiling over
her shoulder and offering a cigarette.
"West" cigarettes, some huge joke on all
of us, as if the unbound breasts were
some great gift to the innocent "East."
In one version her arms are stiff,
in the other relaxed, but in both

she looks for all the world
like she'll have nothing of the man
who offers her a cigarette. She purses
her tiny pink lips and thrusts her regal
nipples into the close air of the underground,
and the train, like the curtains in my head,
the curtains in the heads of all women
who pass this way, close over her nakedness
till only the merwoman's tiny waist poured
into its jade fishtail is left
framed in the train window.

Glimpse of Germania Near Teufelsberg

Berlin, du deutsche deutsche Frau
Ich bin Deine Hochzeitsfreier
Ach, deine Hände sind so rauh
von Kälte und von Feuer.

Wolf Biermann

The door of her Grunewald *Laube* is open
and she a silhouette against the slim
monument of light from the other side.
I no longer think of her as one
of my mothers; she's too sleek
in the linen dress, open at the seams
of each gore, and smaller than I'd guessed.
She speaks to someone I can't see
in a language I didn't know I'd need.
Even now I pull only edges from the weave
of grammar and noise, nouns, verbs
in their glittering necklace of smaller
words, conjunctions, prepositions still
clinging to a rush of oblivious similarity.
But how precise her lips are,
forming words I begin to see
as she eats the light behind her.
I am not her child and almost done
wishing to be. I have no smell
by which she could know me as her own,
but I've walked the map of spilled
blood under her smooth bodice
and watched the veins heal new paths
like those in the limbs of wounded cats.
Now her heart inclines north and east
as in the human breast, beneath
the river of dust where she was slit
from crown to heel— *Das Land der Mitte*—
'heart' as even the American president said,
but if I could see her eyes right now,
there would be fear, the Great Fear.
Though her dress is from the south, cosmopolitan,
Czech flax, Italian seams, and though she's travelled
there, everywhere, in fact, on this unrolled

49

bolt of earth, she always returns to this
moment, this wood where autumn lies down first
and longest, where rubble from the last war
was enough to make a mountain
on which the evening's shadows
are enormous, and very red.

My Mother Watches Me Until the Train Comes In

She has come to Berlin to watch me be
what she never could, independent woman
in an exotic city. She stands at the window,
gauze curtains parted around her like veils,
her whole figure leaning into the hope of seeing me
across Stutgarterplatz and two train platforms.
Though I have walked away from the perils
of this city for two months without her,
tonight she wants to protect me
with her watching. I know that my father
there behind her in the hotel room,
sipping the good Merlot he found cheap
and watching American news, will tell her
to leave me be, that I don't need
mothering. She'll think of sitting down
on the strange hard bed with its feather
pillows punched in the centers so their edges
fly up like wings or starched hats,
and she'll persist in being afraid for me
of this odd country covered in barbed words,
the bratwurst vendor on the street today
whose barrage of German flustered my father
and banished us all to the island of each other again.

The Zoo train rattles the edge of darkness,
drags its beads of light in, then out again.
I stand in the drizzle and look at my mother
framed in the window of the Charlottenburg Hof,
just above Cafe Voltaire and the Starlight Lounge
where beautiful Asian girls stand in the doorways,
naked under their leopard print coats.

And what have you been doing here, dear?
my mother asks over dinner, when it seems
my father and I are about to argue ourselves
apart over the relative kindness of capitalism.
I have been, I tell her, *walking.*
Just walking? she asks. *Yes.*
How can I tell her I have been trying
to walk away from my own tedious self,

the ignorance and otherness that cling to me
like a much-worn dress. I walk to erase
the borders of unknowing, to elude
an old dream of myself. And still I know
little more than which cafe has the last sun,
where to find figs, English papers, silk blouses,
the best fish soup. She understands,
my once and still beautiful mother
at the window. For one moment she wants
to join me, to feel my skirt against her knees,
to move bravely through the foreign night,
untying all the ropes.

The rain is so small its drops stick
like pollen, now chill, now balm.
I want to wave at my mother in her window
worrying the night to shreds for me,
but I'd blow my cover as self-assured
European woman, so well disguised
I'm even asked when or where the next
train goes. And I know. I tell the young woman
carrying a cello that the next train goes
to Westkreuz. I want to follow her,
ask her where she is going with that wonderful
black-suited instrument, but if I move
my mother can no longer watch me—
and it seems important to lend her my life
for a moment because she finds it glamorous
and free, because it might be safe,
now that she's old, to let her wander
in my paper house.

This afternoon she took in and approved,
as if it were her own, my writing room,
my view of the lake, gift of a country
I've tried so hard to know. I've read
its history, taken a few of its spitting words
into my soft mouth. I've looked into
its windows, rivers, and dark paintings.
I've stepped into its ceremonies, town halls,

trains and blue cafes, felt the cool breath
of its endless guilt on my shoulder.

It will be a long wait at Westkreuz
for the next train, and I will sit
in the splintered cradle of a bench there,
breathing the smoke of a man with a black
briefcase, his jaw muscle twitching.
What dangers does my mother imagine for me
in this affluent and orderly country
where no one will cross a street without
the green cartoon of permission?
What perils that I have not been offered
in my own country, each of the cities
I tried to lose myself in before she came
to rearrange the shadows, to tidy my rooms
and touch the spines of all my books,
to cover me at night with her cloying love.

I am free to resist her there in the window,
to move aside so she cannot find
my shape from where she stands—
but I don't move. I can't.
I stand here giving myself to her
as long and as perfectly as I can.

Your Window on the Wannsee is Closed

For Fritz

But mine is open, the water unappeased
as if asleep in a troubled glass. Our trees

refuse their leaves because the moon
carves your name in the sore sky,

and the swans tuck their white heads
into glowing wings. Tiny wild pigs huddle

beneath the forest in sleep. Yellow willows
wash their hair in the lake you could see

from your bed if you woke with me
and I fell over you like words on a page

of days not yet written, a skiff of fictions
without anchor. A thought lifts from my hand

like the gull spilling circles on the lake
as it kicks and shatters the slaked surface.

What did you want before you saw my face?
The rain sounds like paper crushed in a fist.

My terror holds its breath for us.
Trees preen in the rain. Sorrow is so pink.

The spilled hill soaks in spring,
my belly, my hips, my breasts soaked.

That blue rift in the sky with ragged edges
is the shape of the place you tore

from my throat to my knees
with your tongue. Before you spoke to me

my spirit was so small it rode in a locket
hung on the neck of a purely painted girl.

Now white boats bear my sadness away and far.
Somewhere up the lake and down a river

they will people a village with my exiled griefs,
send them on to meet me in a cold city

on another continent. Some silly song in my womb.
Clouds scatter and blend. Fruit weeps in my hand.

Your one window on the Wannsee is dark and high,
a page of wishes the bare trees read to the sky.

My Father's Socks Go Abroad

My dear, did you change your stockings?
                    Mr. Woodhouse, Emma

I've left them with ticket stubs and phone numbers
in rooms in half a dozen countries, taken away
instead small souvenirs, soaps and maps, coins
with the faces of queens, lizards and lions.

Navy, brown and black cotton wools,
green grids of reinforcement over the toes
and heels, the wear at the ball of his foot
inched under the higher arch in mine.

Like Europe's pension rooms, they were never all
that warm, but spacious. In them I climbed the shelves
of bell towers, and paced the *Platz* before the *Frauen-*
kirche where a cold spritz of rain waited with me

for a tardy lover. Evening cleared the square, crawled
up the cool cobblestones to the locked door of the closed
church. Bells rang elsewhere and fountains stopped.
Shops locked up while I tried to believe he'd arrive.

It was my job to rip them, hissing with static,
apart when they came from the dryer, to match
them, blues and blues, blacks and blacks, cull
for thinness and file them in the father

drawer with his mustache scissors and buried copies
of *Last Tango in Paris* and *Fanny Hill*.
When they were new and tight beneath his leather
shoes, they stayed mostly home in Ohio.

When they were thin, they went into a bag
by the dryer became dust mitts, polishers.
Slipped over the hands and wrists of women,
they made their second life as paws or puppets.

Some of them made it with him all the way to Moscow
and Madrid, Paris and Katmandu, stood patient
by the tour bus as my mother left the bazaar
trailing hawkers and refusing to buy until

they cried. I peeled them off in a dim, high-
ceilinged room on the outskirts of Berlin:
Meines Vaters Socken, I laughed as they came
off for the kissing of my suddenly lovely toes.

How odd, the housekeeper must have thought
in Prague, Rome or Bonn, to find men's socks
among the cotton buds, powder spills, an American
girl for sure in *Zimmer, stanza* or *pokoj* 5,

who must have sent a lover squeaking, sockless
off into the night. And perhaps the woman saved them
again, thought them still good enough to warm the toes
of her own sweet night visitor, whose feet are ever

cold since he came to this country, who goes
through socks like paper as he looks for work
and whispers foreign but oddly familiar words
while he ceremoniously peels each thin sock off,

and she marvels at how the warm soles of the feet
are always yeasty, the palest part of any living
body, how the foot's delicate arch is the only place
she can hold the whole man in the cradle of her hand.

The Small Streets of Ubud

Bali, Indonesia

deepen with moonless rain, with the smell
of white people's food, garlic and cakes,
bread and wine. But the feet of the Balinese
women are quiet, not even the holiest whisper
in attendance to the gods. Under the gloam
of kerosene lamps they cut and sew young
coconut leaves into intricate ribbons
and sprigs of tribute, tighten their hips
and hair for the long walk in the rain.
In this industry of reticence, one raises
a white flower over bent knees, and smoke
wafts the prayer up. She dabs at the wisps
with her blossom to speed its way. Only the gods
know how far she's walked with the tower
of impaled fruits on her head, over the bridges
and in the wide scallops of rice terraces
with their paths thin as membrane and unlit
except for the light in the soles of her feet.

Asia

for Jonathan Holden

So you have buried Asia,
her secrets, her dark eyes,
the wet tag of her hair
stuffed in her mouth.
You think how well
you knew her by those voices
pearling through dreams
like oil through water.
By day you discovered
musky chanting skin.
By night, rustling
and spirals of sand.

But you could not move
into that life or the other.
You waited there, a candle
burning clean until the wind
dropped wax away from you,
and there was no shape
you could identify.

You have come back here,
the carrion of Asia dragging
through your words, but
morality tucked like a rose
between your teeth.
When the poems stop
bleeding in your mouth,
you begin to speak
another language.
The tone is of apology,
and each word
is lopped off, final.

You have chosen a different fruit,
one with a skin you cannot eat,
seeds and a stem. All I had
to do was go on telling you
about the others, the ones

I take apart with my mouth
instead of a knife.

Mark the energy in the sky,
the wind huddled in your path,
dry-eyed and forgiving. Mark
the snow shyly joining dark
water, the welcome erosion
of winter in your own country.

The Keening

It comes into the room after we have all eaten
the good meal, spoken the politenesses.
One of us has even told a funny story,
an intimate story, and everyone loved
the one who told it, how once young he woke
       in a loft with a view of a dark lake,
       lights hovering on its glass face
       and touched the woman he wanted to marry
       to wake and look.

I sit next to the storyteller whose bare
shoulders I see in that lake light as if
I were the woman he touched awake,
and his eyes seem bluer.

It has been an evening of guessed alliances,
a dance of traded darts between the eye
and the heart. Over the boiling rice,
the darkening meat, someone's hand on a spoon
is familiar, full of bewitching sadness.
The guests take turns coming into the kitchen
gazing into the pots, the steamed faces
of women cooking, which remind us of holidays
gone slow, families disbursed like blown milkweed
over the few decades we know. I wear a yellow
       apron and take the handfuls of spring
       blooms from a man with whom I've spent
       no more than five minutes of my life.
       Grace wears a lavender print dress, pearls
       in a circle over one breast, marking
       the place where she hopes something
       enduring will enter.

And when the meal is suddenly a refuse
of picked bones and left crusts,
strawberry puree running pink
over the last hunks of gold cake, Grace looks up,
sighs and wishes there were more food
to mother. Cognac is passed, we retire,

and the first silence falls, a lull
out of which the question comes, a question
about a painting of a dark blue animal
merged in crimson,
      "Jack's," I say, the weight
      of my regret surprising us all
      into silence, a noisy wind
      momentarily stopped over a field.

And all of us look down in the hush
of old sorrow, hear the eerie keening
of each others' fabulous disappointments:
the whoosh of many uninvited guests descending,
a gang of past lovers shouldering into
the warm spread of cognac, lamplight, silence,
and never-agains.

      Mine draws himself into a ball of vexation,
      yanking the lace around a pillow as he speaks
      the trouble between him and me; Grace's touches
      her forbidden shoulder in a small-town bar,
      and heads turn to the arc of light that cleaves them;
      John's ex-wife curls away from him and toward
      a window cracked open on a field of theoretical snow.

The others I cannot see so clearly,
but the silent wail rings and rings
so many hands descending on flesh,
      so many tousled heads falling toward each
      other, a field of grass buffeted by several
      gusts of wind: the seed heads flowing this way
      and that, some bent by sleeping deer,
      some untouched but thin-necked and bound
      to come down sooner or later.

Snow gathers
            in the dark north side of my street,
and coats are brought from the bedroom.
My arms ache with the desire to stay
the departures. Someone caresses and admires
the wood lintel above our heads because his longing
to touch something is overwhelming.
            I cradle the collapse of my cat weaving among
            our feet, bounce him in my arms till he reaches
            for a man, wraps his strong paws on an arm,
            and the room spins and tips before
            the wind of their leaving gusts out,
            the candles lean away from their going.

The women left move back into their bodies,
back into the empty end of their own century,
sigh, smile, and begin their backward dreaming
of moons rising in the thighs of men walking,
walking so casually away.

Gacela of Departed Love

after Lorca

You who collapsed your trellis of bones
against mine, try to send me now

boon, humid blues from black
women. You whose coming woke

all the nights of my winter, leave me
also the sleep of the drugged,

of the damned biting their flowers of bane.
In the glare of our naked waists, we came

to our glistening child and stilled
like murdered birds heaped on snow,

thin runner of blood, rumor of bruised
synthesis over the feathered wound,

garden of my agony, bloom of my stained
mouth in the palm of your gone hand.

I hear the crimson edge of wine spilled
over where ever I lay you down, spilled

over the table, the cloth you brought
to your mouth, brought to my mouth.

Your scars rise like many imploring
fish. They do not swim hard enough

to reach me. I would touch those crossed
stitches. I would mend them again to my hips

of pooled petals, wine spilled into the arch
of your foot. Hush, hush, I hear rain caught

in the small place where baneberry roots,
garden of my agony, bloom of my white

wrist in the din of your gone hand.
Ribbon of only rain, I taste ashes again.

The Suit

In all honesty, I don't recall your tie,
only that there was some flash under the fine
black dress coat, its lapels so costly
they lay steamed and obedient
as airbrushed women. Are your feet
beautiful? Is your mother alive?
Such a suit so late and a weeknight
in the tiny few-tabled artists' bar,
I mistook you for a cellist or baritone
just come from performance. Such
is my faith in the beauty of things.

How disappointing to get you at our table
and find you a hockey player turned
stockbroker who's broken two dates
already this evening, who's left three
marriages and cracked another. You smell
of smoke and your hands are smooth
as piano keys. They flutter at the gold
glass of beer, at the saucy barmaid
you've been chatting up for hours.
How many peaches, paintings, petticoats
do you keep on hand? Is there anything
we should know behind your eyes?

We don't want you, my friend and I,
though it's no secret we're looking
for men— or she is, and I'm assumed
to be because I haven't one. If we
were different women, blonder maybe.
Never married. If we grew marigolds
on terraces or kept Afghan hounds
to match our ottomans.

But you'll never believe we don't
want such an exquisite suit, dimples
and a French darkness around the temples.
Have you a favorite pen in your desk?
Will you give it to me if I ask?
Can we go there now and get it?
Do certain colors frighten you?

Since we don't want you, we choose
to mother you, hear out your story
of the only woman you ever loved,
how many orgasms you and she unleashed
on the world when last you saw her,
the husband she went back to, the wives
you left without ever having loved.

Will you shrink if we talk about your body
as if you're not in it? Would you
be frightened if I wanted to touch
your starched shirt, crush your tapered
lapel between my fingers and relish
the impeccable weft of its wool?
How many hours today have you been this suit?

My friend has lost her husband
to a younger woman, and I,
I have my excuses for feeling unwise.
It's 20 below, we came here to escape
suits like you, to watch the steam freeze
white waves over the tall windows,
to take small comfort in the regulars,
unwashed hair, wet boots, garlic and wax.
We thought your suit said something else,
and then too late, we saw your money clip,
so many crisp hundreds, their zeros leaping
from the stack like hugs without kisses.

How many engines will it take to carry
your confused heart away? How far
will it have to travel before we're
safe again? How many of you are there
on the town tonight? What are our chances
of finding you next door, across the street?
Where did you get that suit? Who is that
suit? Where does it live? How do you keep
it so fine all day? How are, who are,
when can we, should we, why do they, where
are your real hands?

Temporary Services

Memory goes first, the personal
spiral here, why we, they, are all
alive and clean at 8 a.m. and leave
bad backs, confused children, lovers
out there. You'd think one could hold on
to some of it, allow the reel to run
over the fields and box houses we all
must have come from. Red dirt. Thistles.
Didn't we all love them once, or was it
only me who noticed what was blooming?

Once you could buy lizards at fairs,
curled in plastic boxes, a short rein
on each green neck that held it
to the pin. I prized the ones
that tended toward blue to match
my eyes. No one seemed to find this
cruel, though we tired of wearing them,
and they died in drawers of pins
and bottled glue, or escaped into the cool
forest of furniture and heavy draperies.

I am afraid what I love will get away from me
because I do not know a good word for what
keeps it in place, the *ever fixed mark*.
All I can get on the first day is a few
fragments, the ones that rhyme. When the others
go to lunch, I sit at the bank of phones
wearing the tiara of wires that ends
inside my ear. *I never writ* comes first,
then the *admit impediments*.
But all day I am missing the *tempest*.

I can only do it if I think of myself
as an impostor. When he calls me in
to the interior, I pick up my pad,
and smile, because I have only seen this
in movies and am afraid it isn't really
done. He speaks to me with a wave toward
the phone, the heap of filing, baskets

that mean in, out, whatnot, as if I
have been here before. He is mild,
milky, soft somewhere under the costly shirt.

Now it is full summer, the cannas burst
on the gully out back and green lizards
run up the sills. I keep the windows
open at night, but it means sleeping
in sweat. It means the glass breaking
on the curbs will ring through to me,
and the storm of police helicopters
will tremble the sashes, swing the shadows
of the fan blades across the ceiling;
the anchor of my purest thoughts, the nurse.

So I tell myself— *the still, sad music,* so hard
to hear. When they give me an hour of Xeroxing
I play, lay my fingers in the borders, reduced;
the ring I wear, a fish with a garnet eye,
will be filed forever with the phone bills
of doctors from last September. What else.
They don't keep me busy enough, and reading
is forbidden. Yesterday I tried Browning
at lunch: "How They Brought the Good News
From Ghent to Aix," but it wouldn't stay.

Something about horses and spurs, a church
steeple. Two of the horses fell. One lasted
the journey. But the whole thing turned into
the midnight ride, and by 5 I had *one if by land
two...* though I didn't want it. And horses.
Once I wanted one. I cut out pictures of studs
and good brood mares, hung them in my room
with the ones I drew, their eyes too big,
lashed like girls' and swaybacked. Better
than anything, I want one still.

When I wake I will have the argument of birds
and the dust of the back lot on my lips
before the obligatory shower, bra

and slippery dress I find in the back
of the closet from another time like this.
I am surprised I still understand what
is wanted, the detail of the fabric, the voice
we women bring from the bedroom to the desk
where all the phone lines end and no one
gets through without us.

Each morning now I go to the calculator
and take a moment to run my rate of pay
against the hours, remind myself what
I'm worth to them, to this world which is,
after all, substantial. And I am trying to find
a way to take heart in with me, but I see
how the best lines wither under the repetition
of the functional: *Information Services—*
help you. Two days to find out what
they produce here: reams of numbers, words
cold and dry as paper in the mouth.

Today I pick the blue and white
polka dots— just the words *polka dots,*
that's what I hang here, words, a music
that doesn't belong. If I went in his office
and said *polka dots,* what would he do? His wife's
name is *Gardenia.* When I look at him
I think of her in a green dress, moist
white flowers, sachet. *Gardenia.* My mother's
college roommate had that name too,
but I can't say so, *May I take a message?*

Now I have a plan: to memorize sonnets,
to hang them on the side of the computer
where he can't see them. I thought of
leaving them on all the computers I touch,
still might, a mystery file named *Will*
filled with the shreds I've snatched
out of the controlled air. I think
it will be my mission here to leave potent
words, to make them necessary,

but I am afraid they are not.

What have I paid for in the last hour?
The phone call to my mother on Saturday,
the cat's rabies shot, a five-liter box
of wine. It will take a whole week of this
to pay the airfare to New York. How much
does each line cost me? How many times
will I have to say *Information Services*,
to pay the light bill? *I new pay*
as if not paid before. What if
he catches me with the *Will* file open?

I have never been fired from a job
in my life. Good girl. Obedience
is dangerous, which is why I love men
who aren't. Somewhere across the city
is a man who is not amused that I am here,
unavailable to him, obedient to others,
aiding in the production of something
that is not art. *Death is the mother*
of beauty. Out of the board meeting.
No wonder he called it "Sunday Morning."

Sex is more potent than poetry. But look,
there's none of it here. It was first
to go, not memory or the words, but touch,
heat, skin, nerves magnified. There are thirty
men in the offices behind me, and women
roving with folders and messages. Touchless,
for eight hours, shoulders craving cradle,
though at lunch, the elevators crowd,
and we glance each other getting out.
Only then do I smell the bodies wearing down.

There is a view of the city behind me
and certain hours of the day that I now
do without. But dawn and dusk they've left
to us, the primal times when we all
must fall into other arms— *Hurry up please*

it's time. We lock up thousands of signatures,
slide our purses into the light. Drawers snap shut
on thirteen floors, and over our shoulders we sling
what we have: money, medicine, tissues, snapshots,
and keys, *sweet ladies*, keys to the *door*
     of the dreadful tower, below.

Warts

I grew a big one on my thumb. At first
an itchy blister with a white halo,
it clutched a pocket of seeds and intrigued me.
Though I'd seen them roughening the knees,
elbows, knuckles of boys, no girl I knew
had one. So I dug at the tiny fortress
at night till it broke through its first
ring, and scattered pods of dread
down the length of flesh below my thumb.
I was sure it meant I couldn't be loved.

By day I peeled scraps from the top,
by night I gouged at the roots and left
a telltale spatter of picking in my sheets.
For months I tried to hide what I grew
in the dark garrison of my childhood,
asking for Band-Aids too often, complaining
of innocent encounters with stumps, stones,
cats and concrete, but the warts were something
else, unstoppable flowering of my own
wrong stigmata. I sobbed and dreamed
of the rusty shreds in their milky pockets,
wanted to believe I'd simply touched
one toad too many, but kids said toad pee
couldn't *really* do that.

So it was me. Maybe I'd touched myself
too much at night, exploring the strange
heat of my secret nest. I lay for hours
in the tub soaking them white, hoping
they'd drop like scales, hoping I'd become
immaculate and girl enough again. I held
my forefinger tight over the rotten place
on my thumb for all of a year before my mother
noticed and bought the burning liquid
that crackled when it hit the hard hearts
and stripped them to dry, harmless flakes of chalk.

But it was only the tops that came off
and I went to piano lessons ashamed,
holding my monster fingers over the dainty
keys for the teacher's punishing stick.
At last my mother took me, terrified, to the city
to a doctor who gassed my gnarled gardens
till they shriveled. But the roots held,
sprouted every year and joined the swell
of girlish worries: *Where are my promised
breasts, my peaches and cream, my good blood?*

I went on with piano lessons that never took,
cures and silent crushes that didn't either,
and all the time I knew it wasn't done
with me, whatever it was my body
was dredging up in the dark, the burrow
and flourish of armies of unthinkable things,
bones, sores and protrusions, my secret
fields where nothing fair, pure
or girl enough to be loved
could ever grow.

Deutscher Kaffee

for J.P.

I've said it's like a body, bitter
and warm, too strong, and once

you're used to it, no other country
can offer enough. Opaque as well,

like the inner arm of a man
you've been allowed to touch

just enough to brew something
aromatic, *voll*, but a short-lived

pleasure. I've said *heart* but
that's not what hurts when the body

vanishes like light in a tunnel
all at once, before your eyes adjust,

though the radio keeps on with silly
song, and your hands on the wheel

still know where you're going.
There's enough to love in any world

without this body. When you arrive
in its country, you'll drink the sharp

offering like a punishment. No one
kisses on the trains there, and you can't

tell a love song from an elegy. Then,
one year later to the day, you'll happen

to drink the *deutschen Kaffee* a friend has brought
from the city you keep trying to return to.

It tastes like the skin of the nights
you had there, like the mouth of days,

like the man who kept vanishing,
the way they do anywhere

from the small circle of your obstinate
claiming, your drinking at the breath

that is the body, that is the man that is
the music, fickle and troubling and never

enough.

Blood Oranges

The snow cannot be said to be really *falling*.
Rather it dives sideways, drives across
the lake and land until it hits a tree,
a wall, a pane of glass and there immolates
itself. A black crow dives on the understanding
of the wind, falls forward into it, claps
its wings to its sides suddenly smooth as a bullet,
gains speed, then unfolds its wings and pours
itself down the sky. I take a cold blood orange
from my store, ready for the tiny bubble
of ruby juice that will weep from the cut seam.
Thousands of purpling pinpoints mottle
its skin, rusty as a pointillist painting
from a distance. The blood won't pour,
but well up from the blister of fruit-flesh
and slide like a tear over my knuckle.
The lawn below me grows a rind of snow
over the snarled winter dirt— the wind
all a rage. The orange, by contrast, gives up
its blood quietly, gracefully as a girl
rich with inexplicable and dramatic sadness
who draws angels for days, then drags a knife
like a paintbrush across her wrists, to see
how the blood rises and squeezes past
the flaps of her flesh, and to feel
the faint whisper of the next world
before a boyfriend catches her, binds her
wounds and drags her back to this one.
Fruit or flesh, it hardly matters, except
for the way the mind finds beauty in it,
and the hand slices and pushes at the sweet
transparencies to flush pleasure and desire
from their secret pockets— this is all
there is to the inner world, ruby juice.
One moment I hold the opened chambers
in my palm and peel off each tumescent
sector, pushing apart the milky membrane.
This fruit calls for care, lest the blood
escape, stain the inner rind scarlet.

The point was never to obliterate the self,
but to bring it more deeply into being.
Blut Orangen, the Germans call these
so as I hold one delicate wing of fruit
against the storm's white fury, I think
'blut and guts,' a trail of entrails
at nature's white mercy, the heart we must eat
to know. Score the four shallow seams,
guessing always how deep is too deep,
until you wound the fruit precisely,
formally, and see the inner life for what
it is: savor it, sweet and bloody,
roseate, inflamed, momentary marriage
of the wounds the world gives us
and the wounds we give ourselves.

Berlin Hinterhöfe

If there were light, we might have solved
the puzzles of small gray rooms, dusted
off the jagged pieces and put them back
together. That rarity of light so true
it hurt, each corner subtracted by the day
and hour it would fall, or not fall.
Maybe it falls, at noon, out there
in the *hof* only, a blinded space
among the strong shadows of sloped roofs,
window boxes and the fat red heads
of geraniums, where the missing piece
should fit. Someone's glasses turn
opaque in the glare of it: ah the day
she doesn't have to work anymore,
she'll sit in that small rip
of delight, sit and open her eyes
just a slat, not enough to see what's
out there, not enough to let go
of the blood she's watching in her own
eyelids.

And he, the one who hid for years
in a grain bin, knew he could go on:
time was light was there moving the days
through that one splintered welt.
Now he makes a point of riding
the *S-Bahn* in the afternoon, Zoo Station
all the way to Wannsee, and there it will
be on the right going, on the left coming,
and he'll have the luxury of closing his eyes
this time, letting the red ride on his retina.

The luxury of having enough
to shut some out, green blinds and vines
going down over it, the needles of it
between the leaves, between the lines.
And why should it always have been a figure
for divinity if it meant, really, nothing more
than simple happiness one could shut
one's eyes and enjoy. That cathedrals

were built to let it in, but only
over our heads or through the thick
lens of leaded glass, that in the artificial
dusk one would see exactly where
it was all coming from,
and that it was all going toward the gold
leaf on the angels, the starburst tossing
cherubs upward, the heavy baroque stairs
to the pulpit, spilling off the gold
umbrella, the flash of lilies and choir robes,
marbles and wimples, the checkerboard floor.
That it was everywhere taken from us
so we'd remember the lost pieces
so we'd have to close our eyes
if ever we wanted to see ourselves whole.

Die Aufklärung

My first and only real love was Ireland;
naturally, he drank like a fish and left me
to Wales, but Wales was already married
and wouldn't let go. Mexico would have
loved me forever, but he was mad
as a hatter, and I was growing old.
I tried to capture Finland on the rebound
but he was still obsessed with India,
so I fished again across the sea
and caught Germany's eye, but Germany
had no time for me just then and left me
in the company of Latvia, Switzerland
and Austria— whom I promptly adored.
My God, that smile dazzling as a chandelier.
Lobmeyr. Austria, however, only loved me
briefly in a dream. Not the marrying
type, so I took refuge in Prague,
who left me at a party with Indonesia.
Indonesia was sweet, but I was restless,
had a fling with Poland, too young
and unbelievably cruel. Indonesia
waited patiently in Budapest, healed me
with a little yoga and *Selamat Siang*,
but Germany seemed to want me back,
so I went and listened sympathetically
to all his troubles. But by then Hungary
had fallen in love with Rome
after the fiasco in Switzerland.
She bade me come see for myself
how exquisite Rome was. Indeed,
he was a charmer, but not mine.
Still pining for Austria, I gave Germany
one more try, and much to my surprise,
he was available, completely and at last.
Marriage, I know by now, is not
an option, but this could last, it could,
though, of course, Germany still has
some feelings to work out for Africa.

Macet

Jakarta, Indonesia

Macet, they say, traffic jam, and gun it
into a side street where no needy faces push
against the glass, against the bewildered heart
of the American girl in the back seat. I am leaving
Jakarta tonight and want to empty the wads
of damp rupiah from my purse, thirty dollars
perhaps, when I see the boy ahead, pushed
along by a grizzled, featureless man,
pushed because he cannot choose his own way
among the hundred barely rolling tires
that would, so easily, find a blind boy's foot
and stand on it. Of course, this one
has to be comely, but I can't see that
from a distance, only that he's stiff
as a mime, or a man on stilts among the cars
three abreast in one lane and nosing
toward every breath of space. He hugs
a staff between his upper arm and chest,
so he can shove the crushed hat with both hands
toward tinted windows, a few of which might
come down. For me there's too much asking
for attention in the road, a narrow noodle cart
toiling through the gaps, its clack-clack almost
in sync with children chasing and smacking
a gaunt dog in the ditch, the dip and sputter
of a motor bike breaking rank and pouring
pitch over us all. It's only when the boy
comes closer that I see the white pupils,
the gluey discs poked deep in his dark
sweat-polished brow. By the time
they get to us, I'm in damned tears
again, that old burning so slow to come
for those I love, so quick to gather
and fall for public gusts of pain.

My friend whose car this is, is sleeping.
She's told me time and again not to give in
to the street's appeals, that the truly maimed
are always in the service of enterprising
pretenders, in this case, the ugly seeing one,

who will pocket whatever beauty wins,
and the more he makes on the blind
boy, the more others will find and employ
their own ruined children. So I sit tight
and glum in the fume of afternoon and think
only of how lucky the old man is to have found
a pain so pretty it will hurt not to hand
over everything for love of beauty alone.

Give your money, she says, to the cook,
the driver, the maid; buy trinkets, eat
sumptuous meals, make our economy spin
like a wound top— but don't, don't give
so much as a coin here. She's sleeping,
though, when they arrive at our window,
her head fallen against the smoked glass;
and the face of the boy hangs over her dreaming,
framed and magnified, his vacant eyes looking
somewhere higher than where we are, above
her luxuriant drowse, and if right now
I pressed the button that makes the window
whisper down, her head, her dark, fragrant
hair would spill into the blind boy's arms.

Last Year Buddhas Were Big

Ubud, Bali

If there is an overbalance of curiosity, then, we have the grotesque in art: if the union of strangeness and beauty, under very difficult and complex conditions, be a successful one, if the union be entire, then the resultant beauty is very exquisite, very attractive.

"Romanticism," Walter Pater

This year it's stars and moons on strings,
pressed with gold and hung in the weather

to ripen a bit, and there are animal stools,
spotted zebras, grinning frogs, red-mouthed

tigers, horses and bugs upon whose backs
we can sit or prop our feet. Wooden flowers

loll on wooden stems, painted a green
so garish it hurts the eye, if not the soul,

wooden fruits, whole fake banana trees, lemons
with stippled skin and fabricated bruises,

even bunched grapes and saffron apples, much
that never grew here. But no rambutan or durian,

the native fruits that reek and feed a burning
in the gut, only the fabulous hues and joys

of familiar kitsch, a thousand pretty suns
as many smiling moons, cartoons conceived

in the other half of the mind and mirrored here.
I long for beauty in strangeness until I hear the mad

plans of the white woman who advises a village
of young female painters: Oh gracious, not these

garlands and flowers, not these flagrant colors—
these are too tawdry, tame, my dears, express yourselves!

Confused, the young painters wave their brushes
and muter colors over wood, canvas, clay and paper:

This? This? You sell? This one feed
my children? Maybe, says the white woman,

but that is not why you must do it. Art must
turn away from the market and look askance

at the past. Confused, the girls go home and wave
their wands again— babies, shadows, the curves

of mothers, sisters, secrets they never wished
to tell. Ah, yes, says the woman now, your own

body and blood, your own strangeness: this will feed you,
and feed, she thinks, the lust for such across

the sea. And this one, says the woman, unrolling
a gray green field of tiny busy figures, this one

is real, and not for sale because it's traditional
two-dimensional, magic, made with holy water, mine.

When I Come Home From Asia We Are All Hungry

St. Paul, Minnesota

Two of us have lost grandmothers
while the snow, bulldozed into great
sullied chunks, hardened. One of us
has conceived a child and fights regret,
the maimed silence of the man
who in autumn seemed to agree
she could have that garden. One
of us shut her door to the world
and refused to be drawn away
from the small fire of her own
losses— a mother to cancer, three
fathers in varying shades of connection
and disconnection. One of us
lost herself in the ribs of rice
terraces in a rainy season, dispersed
whatever was left of herself into the marvel
of the lung-shaped pools of mud
threaded with new green shoots.

All of us stand at the airport gate
together again for the first time
in a year, drive off into the blue
belly of a January Minnesota night
hungry. In Burger King's coarse
florescence we unfold our packages
of cheap meat, indulge ourselves
in the oily air, and trade our trouble
around: one of us jobless and afraid
she will fall from the edge of having;
one of us offering the feast of the child
the man has pushed away, now ours,
growing among us. We pass it
like an exotic dish, more thrilling
than the white buns lying in shredded
nests of paper before us, more strange
than the rolling eye of the carp
one of us chose and carried away
from the edge of the Java Sea.

We stare down into our translucent
ovals of grease and see the tiny fetus
somersaulting beneath the Formica table,
and the two of us who do not carry
life in our bodies take the idea of it
like a wafer of hope, and pass it down,
down into the empty depths of all
three of us, women in a cold state,
waiting for the hot little fist
of that baby heart to open and astonish us.

Notes on the Poems

"Babes in Toyland": *Chrysolite, beryl, sardius, pearl:* see Revelation, Chapter 21.

"Pandare" : "Pandarus." This spelling is Chaucer's from *Troilus and Criseyde*.

"Kebyar Trompong": Balinese dance form: "the Kebyar dancer presents a range of moods— from coquettishness to bashfulness, and from sweet imploring to anger. . . performed while playing the *trompong* (a long instrument with 14 inverted kettle gongs), using theatrics and flashy moves to coax sound from the instrument." Rucina Ballinger, *Bali.*

"Getting the Naughty Bits of *Bahasa Indonesia*": *Bahasa Indonesia* is the Indonesian national language developed at the beginning of the 20th century by Dutch scholars to facilitate communication among the more than 250 different native languages of the Indonesian archipelago. *Boule* is an Indonesian term for people of European descent.

"At the Bandung Emergency Room": Bandung is in Central Java, Indonesia. *Rumah Sakit* is Indonesian for "hospital."

"Whale Watching": *Ballena* is Spanish for "whale."

"Glimpse of Germania Near Teufelsberg":
> Berlin, you oh so German lass
> I court you with desire
> But oh, your hands are rough, alas
> From cold winds and from fire.

Wolf Bierman, *Poems and Ballads* (trans. Steve Gooch, 1977).

Laube is the German word for small weekend bungalows that line railway tracks and parts of the Grunewald park within which lies *Teufelsberg*, "Berlin's highest (383-foot or 115-metres) point . . . created after the war from 33 million cubic yards (25 million cubic metres) of rubble" (*Berlin Insight Guide*, 110). *Das Land der Mitte*, literally the country in the middle, a sometime epithet for Germany, see Gordon Craig, *The Germans*. President Clinton, visiting Berlin during the summer of 1993 also referred to Germany as the "heart" or middle of Europe.

"Mermaid in the U-Bahn Station": The U-Bahn (short for *(Untegrundrbahn)* is Berlin's underground rail system.

"My Father's Socks Go Abroad": The *Frauenkirche* is the Cathedral Church of Our Lady in Munich. *Zimmer, stanza* and *pokoj* mean "room" in German, Italian and Czech respectively.

"Gacela of Departed Love": After Lorca's "*Gacela Del Amor Imprevisto*" or "Gacela of Unforeseen Love" translated by W.S. Merwin in *Selected Poems of Federico Garcia Lorca*.

"Die Aufklärung": The German term for the 18th-century intellectual movement called, in English, the Enlightenment. See Gordon Craig, *The Germans*: "One of the ideas of the Enlightenment that had been congenial to the educated middle class of the larger states had been that of cosmopolitanism, the view that the cultivated person was a member of a society that transcended national boundaries. Lessing had said that patriotism was not a quality that he coveted, since it 'would teach me to forget that I must be a citizen of the world,' and . . . Friedrich Schiller . . . 'I write as a citizen of the world who serves no prince. At an early age, I lost my fatherland to trade it for the whole world.'"

"Berlin Hinterhöfe": *Hinterhöfe*, back or interior courtyards sometimes as many as five layers deep from the street in Berlin city blocks.

"*Macet*": *Macet* is Indonesian for "traffic jam."

"Last Year Buddhas Were Big": "Cocks and frogs, dressed in resort fashions and armed with Japanese cameras, reflect back the tourists' own image . . . . In staking a claim to creative originality and the vicarious authority of the master. . . [Balinese arts reflect] the conflict between artistic individualism and the values of traditional ateliers and craft communities in which new techniques and ideas were automatically handed on and made available to all" (Anne Richter, *Arts and Crafts of Indonesia*).